KANGAROO

BY TYLER GRADY

Dylanna Press

Kangaroos are **mammals** native to Australia and can be found in a variety of habitats across the Australian continent, including its surrounding islands. They are the largest marsupials in the world and are a national symbol for Australia.

They belong to the Macropodidae family, which literally means "big foot," a nod to their distinctive large feet adapted for hopping. Kangaroos are closely related to wallabies, wallaroos, and quokkas.

Their scientific classification includes several species, with the most well-known being the Red Kangaroo (*Macropus rufus*), Eastern Grey Kangaroo (*Macropus giganteus*), Western Grey Kangaroo (*Macropus fuliginosus*), and the Antilopine Kangaroo (*Macropus antilopinus*). These species vary in size, color, and habitat preferences but share common adaptations for jumping and grazing.

---

mammals – warm-blooded animals characterized by having hair or fur, giving birth to live offspring, and typically producing milk to feed their young.

Kangaroos are muscular and agile, with a powerful build that includes a tapered torso and a long, strong tail used for balance. They vary significantly in size depending on the species, with the larger species like the Red Kangaroo weighing up to 200 pounds (90 kg) [range from 40 to 200 pounds (18 to 90 kg)]. Males are typically larger and more muscular than females. They stand up tall on their hind legs, reaching heights of 3 to 8 feet (0.9 to 2.4 meters) from head to toe, with a length that can include a tail nearly as long as their body.

Their heads are small in proportion to their bodies. They have large, powerful hind legs that dominate their physique and short front legs with **dexterous** paws that they use for eating food and grooming. Their snout is elongated with large ears that can swivel to detect sounds.

Kangaroos' long, powerful tails are not just for balance. They also serve as a third leg to prop them up in a sitting position. Their back feet are large and strong, adapted for leaping, with a distinctive arrangement of toes that aids in their movement. Their fur varies in color from light grey to reddish-brown, depending on the species, and is generally soft and woolly.

---

dexterous – skillful and agile

Kangaroos are **terrestrial** animals that thrive in the varied landscapes of Australia, ranging from open grasslands and deserts to forests and bushland. They are predominantly found in areas that offer both open spaces for feeding and dense vegetation for shelter and protection from predators.

Grasslands and open savannahs are among the most common **habitats** for kangaroos, providing the ideal combination of open space for grazing and areas of brush or woodland for shelter. In these environments, kangaroos can be seen in large groups, known as mobs, which offer safety in numbers against potential threats.

Their habitats include the arid and semi-arid plains of the interior, known as the outback, where vegetation is sparse and water sources are limited. Here, kangaroos rely on their ability to travel long distances to find food and water, often moving at night to avoid the extreme heat of the day.

The diversity of habitats that kangaroos occupy reflects their versatile feeding habits and social structures, allowing them to thrive across a continent marked by extreme weather conditions and varied topography.

___

terrestrial – found on land
habitat – specific natural environment where a particular species of plant or animal lives and thrives

Kangaroos have many physical **adaptations** to their environment.

- **Powerful Hind Legs:** Their long and muscular hind legs enable them to leap more than 30 feet (9.1 meters) in one hop! This allows for rapid movement across open landscapes and escaping predators.
- **Long Tail:** Their strong, long tails are used for balance while moving and can support their body weight when sitting or standing.
- **Large Feet**: Adapted for powerful leaping and efficient movement across various terrains. Each foot has a long fourth toe that acts like a spring, helping them push off the ground with great force.
- **Thick Fur:** The fur of kangaroos provides insulation from both the heat and cold, helping them to regulate body temperature in varying climates.
- **Position of Eyes and Ears:** The ears of kangaroos can swivel to detect sounds from various directions, enhancing their awareness of predators. Their eyes are positioned on the sides of their heads, giving them a wide field of vision to monitor for threats.
- **Teeth:** Kangaroos have sharp front **incisors** for cutting through grass and strong back molars that are well-suited for grinding and chewing tough plants.
- **Digestive System:** A two-chambered stomach allows them to ferment tough plant materials and efficiently extract nutrients. Their slow digestive process also allows for maximum water absorption enabling them to go for weeks without drinking water.

Together, these adaptations enable kangaroos to thrive across the diverse and often challenging landscapes of Australia.

---

adaptations – ways in which a species becomes fitted into its natural environment to increase its chance of survival

incisors – front teeth used for cutting

ferment – process in which a substance breaks down into a simpler substance

Kangaroos are **herbivores** that primarily consume a variety of grasses, along with leaves, flowers, and occasionally shrubs and young shoots. They are not particularly picky eaters but will graze on the most nutritious and available vegetation they can find.

Kangaroos typically spend a significant portion of their day **foraging** for food. They are most active during the cooler parts of the day, such as early morning and late evening, to avoid the intense heat and sun of the Australian midday.

Kangaroos have an efficient digestive system featuring a chambered stomach. This system allows them to break down tough plant materials, enabling them to extract maximum nutrients from their diet.

Kangaroos do not need to drink water very often. In fact, they can go weeks and even months without it! Kangaroos get most of the moisture they need from the plants they eat.

---

herbivores – animals that only eat plants

foraging – wandering around in search of food

Kangaroos

are very social creatures that often gather in groups known as mobs. These mobs can vary in size, typically ranging from a few individuals to over a hundred, depending on the availability of food and water. Within these groups, you'll find kangaroos of all ages and both genders, with one dominant male. The group provides safety in numbers from predators.

In these mobs, kangaroos engage in various social behaviors. They're often seen grazing together peacefully. Adult kangaroos also take turns watching out for potential dangers, such as dingoes or humans, alerting the group with distinct thumping sounds or other vocal signals if threats are detected.

They communicate through a range of sounds from grunts to clicks, and mothers have a special soft clucking sound they use to talk to their joeys. Body language also plays a huge part in their interactions, including boxing or play-fighting, which is common among males practicing their fighting skills or establishing dominance.

Living in a mob helps kangaroos not only to protect each other but also to form strong social bonds that are vital for their survival in the sometimes harsh Australian landscape.

Kangaroos are not particularly **territorial**, but they do establish home ranges where they spend most of their time. These home ranges can vary widely in size, often overlapping with those of other kangaroos. The size and stability of these areas primarily depend on the availability of food and water, which can change with the seasons.

Rather than defending a specific territory from others, kangaroos are more likely to share grazing areas peacefully with other members of their mob. However, males may become competitive and even fight during mating season to establish dominance or win the attention of females.

territorial – animals that guard or defend an area

Kangaroos are primarily active during the cooler parts of the day, specifically at dawn and dusk, making them crepuscular animals. They spend their active hours feeding and socializing, while the hottest parts of the day are typically reserved for resting and digesting their food. Kangaroos do not follow a strict sleep schedule but rather take multiple short naps throughout the day, waking if they sense any danger.

Kangaroos do not use or create shelters like burrows or nests. Instead, they rest and sleep in open areas, often lying down on the grass during the day to rest, digest their food, and stay cool. At night, they are more active, feeding and moving around more freely. Their resting habits help them avoid the extreme heat of the day and reduce the risk of predation, as they can spot approaching predators more easily in open spaces.

Kangaroos are highly adaptable and can modify their activity patterns based on environmental conditions, such as changes in the weather or the presence of predators. In regions where human presence or predator activity is more pronounced, kangaroos may alter their behavior to be more nocturnal, thus staying safer under the cover of darkness.

Their ability to remain alert even while resting is crucial for their survival, allowing them to quickly respond to threats. This vigilance, combined with their social structure where some members of the group stay alert while others rest, helps kangaroos effectively manage risks in their environment, find food, and cope with varying conditions.

Kangaroos are **polygamous**, with dominant males often mating with several females. Kangaroos can breed year-round, but the peak breeding season typically aligns with spring and early summer when food and water are more plentiful.

Male kangaroos, called "bucks" or "boomers," attract females through scent marking and displays of strength, engaging in boxing matches to establish dominance.

Female kangaroos, known as "does" or "flyers," generally give birth to one baby kangaroo at a time, but sometimes twins are born. The gestation period for kangaroos is relatively short, lasting about 30 to 40 days.

Kangaroos are **marsupials**, which means they carry and nurse their young in a pouch after birth. This unique feature allows their underdeveloped newborns, called joeys, to continue growing and developing in a safe, protected environment until they are ready to explore the outside world.

---

polygamous – having more than one mate
marsupials – mammals that carry their young in a pouch

Newborn kangaroos are very small and helpless when born. Babies are only about an inch (2.5 centimeters) in length—roughly the size of a jellybean! They are blind and hairless and immediately seek the safety of their mother's pouch.

The joey remains in the pouch for about six to eight months, during which time it grows rapidly, gaining fur and strength. After this period, the joey starts venturing out, nibbling on grass and leaves, but still returning to the pouch for safety and to nurse.

Kangaroo mothers are attentive and nurturing, watching over their young closely. They teach them how to graze, avoid predators, and interact with other kangaroos. In larger mobs, several mothers may help look after the joeys, creating a supportive communal environment.

By 18 months baby kangaroos are mature and independent. Female kangaroos will stay and live in the same mob as their mothers. Young male kangaroos will eventually leave their birth mob and join other groups or establish their own territories.

Kangaroos play an important role within their **ecosystems**.

Grazers: Kangaroos spend much of their time grazing. This grazing maintains the balance of plant species, prevents overgrowth, and creates space for new plants to emerge.

Seed Dispersers: As they roam and graze, their droppings help to spread seeds and bring plants to new areas, increasing plant diversity. Their dung also enriches the soil and provides food for beetles and other insects.

Food Chain: Kangaroos are a key part of the food chain, providing food for predators such as dingoes and eagles. This predation is a key aspect of the natural food chain, helping to maintain ecological balance.

_____

ecosystem – community of living organisms interacting with each other and their physical environment within a specific area or habitat

The average lifespan of a kangaroo varies by species, but typically, they live around 6 to 8 years in the wild. In captivity, they can live longer, often reaching up to 20 years.

Kangaroos are abundant in Australia and are not currently considered a threatened species. This demonstrates their adaptability and resilience in various habitats across Australia.

The total **population** of kangaroos is around 45 million and has been increasing each year. The conservation status of kangaroos varies by species but is generally listed as "Least Concern" by the International Union for Conservation of Nature (IUCN).

---

population – the members of a species that live in an area

Kangaroos are large animals and have few natural **predators**. Their primary predators are dingoes. These are wild dogs native to Australia and often hunt in packs, allowing them to take down large prey, including adult kangaroos.

Wedge-tailed eagles are large birds of prey that target young or injured kangaroos. With keen eyesight and powerful talons, wedge-tailed eagles swoop down from above to catch their prey.

Smaller and younger kangaroos are also at risk from predators like red foxes, which are non-native to Australia but have spread across the continent, and feral cats, which can be formidable hunters. Additionally, larger reptiles like pythons occasionally prey on smaller kangaroos.

Kangaroos have developed various defenses against these predators, such as their powerful hind legs, forepaws, claws, and teeth. When chased, kangaroos will often head into the water to avoid attack. Their tendency to stay in groups also offers some protection against potential threats. Additionally, kangaroo mothers keep their young in their pouches for protection, while adult kangaroos rely on their keen senses to detect approaching predators.

---

predator – an animal that hunts another animal for food

Aside from predators, kangaroos face several threats and challenges from humans, impacting their populations and habitats:

- **Hunting:** Kangaroos are hunted for their meat and hides, a practice regulated in some areas but still a significant threat in others.

- **Habitat Loss:** Human activities such as urban development, agriculture, and deforestation destroy or fragment kangaroo habitats. This habitat loss forces kangaroos into smaller areas, leading to increased competition for food and water and making them more vulnerable to predators.

- **Road Accidents:** Kangaroos often wander onto roads, leading to accidents that are dangerous for both the animals and drivers. Road construction through kangaroo habitats increases the likelihood of such collisions, posing a serious threat to kangaroo populations.

- **Fencing:** Fences used for livestock and property boundaries can hinder kangaroo movements and access to food and water. Some fences trap or injure kangaroos, while others limit their natural migration patterns, impacting their ability to survive during droughts or seasonal changes.

- **Climate Change:** Climate change poses a threat to kangaroos by altering their environments. Increased temperatures, changes in rainfall patterns, and more frequent extreme weather events can impact food and water availability, stressing kangaroo populations.

- **Conflict with Agriculture:** Kangaroos are sometimes seen as pests by farmers because they compete with livestock for grazing land and water. This can lead to culling or other measures to reduce kangaroo populations, which can be detrimental to their survival.

Despite these challenges, conservation efforts, regulated hunting, and public awareness can help mitigate the impact of human activities on kangaroo populations. Protecting their habitats and understanding the ecological roles they play are key to ensuring their continued survival.

Kangaroos are more than just iconic animals in Australia. They hold a significant place in the country's cultural identity and natural heritage. As national symbols, kangaroos are prominently featured on Australia's coat of arms and currency, reflecting their importance to the nation's history and identity.

In the future, kangaroos face a range of challenges from human activities, including habitat loss, hunting, and climate change. However, with thoughtful conservation efforts, sustainable management practices, and increased public awareness, it is possible to protect these remarkable animals and ensure they continue to thrive. Kangaroos have shown great resilience and adaptability, and with proper stewardship, they can continue to play a vital role in Australia's ecosystems.

The future of kangaroos hinges on the balance between development and conservation. By valuing and safeguarding their habitats, humans can coexist with kangaroos, preserving their cultural significance and ecological importance for generations to come.

---

conservation – the act of protecting ecosystems and environments to protect the animals that live there

Word Search

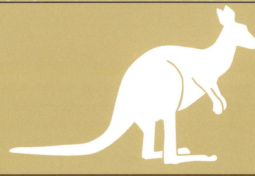

```
E N Y D F O O D C H A I N I O
R O T E M D A Z O Z C T J O C
O I E X C A N B S U N P R R S
V T R T E H M S U E T A O Y K
I A R E G L E M M C G B E C O
B T I R L O V N A N K O A D R
R P T O D Z O U A L J S Z C Q
E A O U B P K I K S Z T V K
H D R S I N O I T A L U P O P
K A Y V K M T H O P C S H F
K Z N A J D G N I Z A R G C O
G E K W K H T G O K P S M U R
G L M A R S U P I A L K O O A
Z B D H P H A B I T A T B P G
N C A I L A R T S U A O S S E
```

ADAPTATION	FORAGE	MAMMALS
AUSTRALIA	GRAZING	MARSUPIAL
BUCKS	HABITAT	MOBS
DEXTEROUS	HERBIVORE	OUTBACK
DOES	HOP	POPULATION
ENVIRONMENT	JOEYS	POUCH
FOOD CHAIN	KANGAROO	TERRITORY

INDEX

adaptations, 5, 10, 18
agriculture, 31
Australia, 5, 9, 27, 32
body language, 14
breeding, 21
climate change, 31
communication, 14
diet, 13
digestive system, 10, 13
dingoes, 24, 28
eagles, 24, 28
ears, 10
ecosystem, 24, 32
environment, 9, 18
eyes, 10
feet, 6, 10
fencing, 31
food chain, 24
fur, 6, 10
grasslands, 9
grazers, 24
habitat, 5, 9, 31
herbivores, 13
hind legs, 6, 10
humans, 18, 31
hunting, 31
joeys, 21, 22
lifespan, 27

mammals, 5
Marcopodidae family, 5
marsupials, 5, 21
mating, 17, 21
mobs, 9, 14, 17, 22
offspring, 21, 22
outback, 9
physical adaptations. *see* adaptations
physical characteristics, 6, 10
population, 27
predators, 14, 18, 24, 28
reproduction, 22
road accidents, 31
savannahs, 9
scientific classification, 5
seed dispersal, 24
size, 6
sleep, 18
social behavior, 14
species, 5
stomachs, 10, 13
tails, 6, 10
teeth, 10
territory, 16–17
threats, 28, 31, 32
water, 13
weight, 6

Published by Dylanna Press an imprint of Dylanna Publishing, Inc.
Copyright © 2024 by Dylanna Press
Author: Tyler Grady
All rights reserved. No part of this publication may be reproduced, stored in a retrieval system, or transmitted by any means, including electronic, mechanical, photocopying, or otherwise, without prior written permission of the publisher.

Although the publisher has taken all reasonable care in the preparation of this book, we make no warranty about the accuracy or completeness of its content and, to the maximum extent permitted, disclaim all liability arising from its use.

Printed in the U.S.A.

Made in the USA
Columbia, SC
26 June 2025